ADVENT/
CHRISTMAS
~ READING ~
REFLECTIONS

For Individuals or Small Groups

ARMAND BRUNELLE, III

Print ISBN: 979-835094-793-9
ebook ISBN: 979-8-35094-794-6

Printed in the United States of America

TABLE OF CONTENTS

PREFACE

I have had the good fortune to be involved in youth ministry for 35 years and Men's ministry for about 20 years. When we first started doing Men's Group, we would meet during Lent and Advent for 6 weeks and simply read the scripture readings for the upcoming Sunday Mass and discuss them amongst ourselves. Usually in groups of 6 to 12 men.

We would ask questions such as what are the readings saying to you? What is the message here? How can we apply this to our life, our world today.

I never had prepared reflections of my own for those meetings; everything was just spontaneous for us and off the cuff. I never took notes either, but the conversations were always great! When I went to Mass that weekend, I was very prepared and even curious to see what Father was going to say to the parish about the readings and how would his remarks align or not align with our thoughts.

During the pandemic when we were unable to go to Mass, I was reading the scriptures for Mass prior to watching the Mass on the computer. Like previously with the Men's Group reflections, I started to think I wonder what Father will say about these readings? One day I just decided to write down in a note on my iPhone what I was thinking and that's how this came to be.

Each Sunday morning after morning prayer with my coffee and my dogs I would read the readings and then jot down my thoughts. I have done this for every Sunday and some Holy Days for Years A, B and C. This booklet is just for the Lenten Sundays for all three years. I have indicated some of the upcoming years so you can align with the current Liturgical Year that we are in as you use this booklet.

So "By what authority do you…?" (Mark 11:28) **I have no authority**. I have not been trained in theology, these are simply my thoughts. If you care to know more about me and my background you can go to the back of the book.

HOW TO USE
THIS BOOKLET

I envision that you could use this book on your own to prepare for Mass but I think it would be better if you can gather with even just a couple of friends. "wherever two or more are gathered in my name there I shall be!" – Matthew 18:20

I would suggest that Jesus is with you too even when you are alone with your Bible.

Our groups would typically have an hour time limit which usually was enough time. Sometimes we went over but I really tried to keep it within an hour to respect everyone's time.

Start by reading the scriptures listed for the day you are studying. You will see them just under the title of the section for that weekend. Hopefully you can decipher my abbreviations for the books of the Bible. I list the first reading from the Old Testament, the Psalm, the second reading from the New Testament and the Gospel for that particular Sunday.

If you are in a group, pick a person to read the scripture aloud. Ideally, you would have a different person read aloud for the other readings.

What follows is my thoughts on what the readings were saying to me when I wrote them. You may agree or disagree with what I have and that is more than okay! The idea is to get YOU thinking about what they are saying to you and your group.

I have included a blank page after my reflections for you to write your own ideas. You could write it in paragraph form as I did or simply put in some bullets or key points that you'd like to remember.

What is nice about doing that is the next time the Liturgical year comes along in three years you can see what you thought back then and see if you still feel the same or hopefully maybe you have grown and have a new direction for the readings and your life!

Either way I hope you find this booklet useful and you come to know God, his son Jesus Christ and their Holy Spirit a little more intimately. That is what its all about! God bless you and your small group!

BREAKING OPEN
THE WORD

It is currently Advent of Year B, December of 2023. I am using a daily devotional booklet by Father Richard Rohr and just came across this essay for December 18th entitled Breaking Open the Word. The readings for December 18th are from Jeremiah 23:5-8 and Matthew 1:18-25. I am hoping that Fr. Richard and the cac.org won't mind me sharing this with you. I have properly footnoted the text and have not changed anything in his essay. Enjoy!

We have a lot to learn from people like Quakers and Mennonites. They are well practiced in being a minority. They don't need to have crowds around them to believe that it is the truth. They gather in little groups and share the Word of God. And that, thank God, is what is also happening again in the Catholic church. We call them "base communities" of Latin America or the Bible study groups of America and Europe. Breaking open the Word of God cannot depend on people like me, theologians or people who have studied professionally. If that would be true, then 99 percent of humanity will never have access to God's Word.

These faith-sharing groups are directed not by a professional teacher or an expert, but rather what we call a facilitator or animator – one who holds the group together and knows what questions to ask to keep people searching and praying. The groups read a Gospel text, sometimes three times and then they ask questions: What threatens them in the text? What makes them excited about the text? What is really challenging in that text? What do they think Jesus was really talking about? What was the world situation when Jesus told that particular story? Are there any comparable situations today to which this text might apply? Or perhaps in today's Gospel, "Do you really think Joseph understood what was happening? Was his trust in Mary, his dreams and the visions of angels really total certitude? Or was it actually faith?" Such questions are allowed and encouraged.

Whatever gave us the idea that one little select group of similarly educated people would best understand what God was to all people? The Word of God is being given back to the poor. The Word of God is being given back to the uneducated and the imprisoned. The Word of God is being given back to women. The Word of God is being given back to non-celibates (for us in the Catholic church). The Word of God is being given back to someone other than those who are employees of the religious system. What we are finding is the Word of God is being read with a vitality, a truth and often a freedom that is exciting, much more challenging and often making us wonder if we have ever understood it before. Just try it. This will not lessen the authority of the church or the Scriptures, but only increase it because we will have spiritual adults in our midst. Spiritual adults do not overreact or think dualistically, but the listen and learn and grow.[1]

1 Preparing for Christmas with Richard Rohr – Daily Meditations for Advent pg 52-54 – 2008 St Anthony Messenger Press Cincinnati, Ohio. Visit cac.org to order your own copy!

LITURGICAL YEARS

The Catholic church organizes its liturgies into three distinct Liturgical Years – Year A, Year B and Year C. When Year C completes, the Church goes back to Year A and then on to Year B after the completion of A and so on. For more information on Liturgical Years please visit the US Catholic Bishop's website: https://www.usccb.org/prayer-worship/liturgical-year

The Liturgical Year starts with the Season of Advent which begins in November of a given year. Below you will find the Liturgical Year Designations for the calendar years through 2031.

Year A
- 2022 (Advent) – 2023
- 2025 – 2026
- 2028 - 2029

Year B
- 2023 (Advent) – 2024
- 2026 – 2027
- 2029 - 2030

Year C
- 2024 (Advent) – 2025
- 2027 – 2028
- 2030 - 2031

FIRST SUNDAY OF ADVENT - YEAR A

Is 2:1-5; Ps122; Rom 13:11-14; Mt 24:37-44

We kick off this new liturgical year A on the First Sunday of Advent with what seems to be a stark warning in our gospel from Matthew. "Two men are out in the field, one is taken one is left. Two women working the mill one will be taken one will be left. Therefore Stay awake! For you do not know the hour that the Lord will come."

Yikes! I don't know about you but I don't want to be the one guy left! Can you imagine that? The glorious coming of the Lord in the Eastern sky and he takes your friend or co-worker and says "sorry".

Isn't that our initial feeling fear of being left? But why would we feel this way? What makes us think that we will be the one left? Probably because we think we are not worthy of the Lords presence. Actually the Eucharistic liturgy reminds us of that unworthiness just before we receive communion "Lord I am not worthy that you should enter under my roof but only say the word and my soul will be healed."

And there is the key! The Lord can just say the word and we will be healed and taken on that day instead of being left.

Truth is we can't earn our way to heaven. Ultimately we have to do our best to hear the gospel each week apply it to our lives and help God bring about his kingdom here on earth. We won't get it right all the time maybe not even some of the time. All we can do is use the talents God has given us to bring more to know him so that they will be taken up too.

That's our job. To share our faith the best we can with family and friends so that more can know the peace of knowing Jesus and can feel confident that the Lord is there for them too and when he comes we will all be counted not because we are worthy but because we recognized Gods presence in our life and was open to His grace.

As we start this Advent season let's do an inventory of the actions Paul lists in the second reading and see what we might do to be more selfless. All those things he lists are selfish things, pleasurable things maybe, but they won't bring us happiness and peace.

We are on the right track because we are here. As our Psalm today says "Let us go rejoicing to the house of the Lord." It is here each week that we learn the lessons of selflessness that Christ teaches us and how we learn to surrender all our fears to God and trust in his mercy and grace.

Do not be afraid of the coming of the Lord! Rejoice because He has called you. Let's help others recognize that He is calling them too maybe through us.

This space is for you to record your comments or your groups comments

SECOND SUNDAY OF ADVENT - YEAR A

Is 11:1-10; Ps 72; Rom 15:4-9; Mt 3:1-12

In our gospel from Matthew today we hear about John the Baptist. A very curious and interesting man I believe even within his time but certainly and odd guy within our time. He wore Camel's hair clothing that sounds itchy to me; He ate locusts and wild honey; the honey sounds good but eating insects doesn't sound good to me; and he lived simply in the desert away from everyone.

A long time ago I remember learning that the word for "holy" in Yiddish translates to odd or different. John sounds pretty odd and Holy to me and do we notice he attracted all kinds of people to the Jordan for his Baptism for the repentance of sins.

He welcomes and offers the Baptism to everyone but we hear that he challenges the Pharisees and Sadducees that if they are truly committed to this Baptism then they must show evidence of their repentance and produce good fruit (good works).

This is the message for me today. I'm like the Pharisees. I go to Mass each week, I do the right things that I am instructed to do. But do I do it in a way that is humble? Or am I doing it for show? Look at me how holy I am! Do I recognize that it is God who has given me the grace to do this? Do I offer those graces back to him through almsgiving, Justice and love of neighbor?

Truly this Baptism of John's is the precursor to Christ's Church's Baptism where we are baptized not just with water but with the recognition of the presence of the Holy Spirit within the sacrament.

Our Baptism, if we honor it properly, comes with a mission and stuff to do like John tells the Pharisees. We must change from our selfish ways to be more selfless.

We are also called to tell others about Jesus and the Holy Spirit and to as Paul tells us in the second reading from Romans to live in harmony with one another. If we truly recognize God in our Baptism and our lives we must repent (in Greek change our minds) which will change how we live.

Isaiah and the Psalm 72 is all about that justice. That is the key about Baptism in Christ. Our mission is to inform others and treat all with justice. To be selfless and caring. That's kinda "odd" in our day where everyone is selfish and concerned about themselves. I too certainty worry about me and my family before everyone else but this Baptism of ours is calling us to go deeper to do more. We need to continue to be more selfless and just.

If we accept our mission of Baptism I reckon we should and will be seen as odd like John.

Hopefully like John we will attract people by our oddness because they will see a peace that permeates our talk and actions. A peace that they will want to share in. A peace that only Christ can bring into our lives.

Come Lord Jesus! Send us your Spirit renew the face of the Earth!

This space is for you to record your comments or your groups comments

SOLEMNITY OF THE IMMACULATE CONCEPTION - YEAR A

Gen 3:9-15,20; Ps 98; Eph 1:3-6, 11-12; Lk 1:26-38

As a kid I always thought that the Solemnity of the Immaculate Conception was about the conception of Jesus within the womb of Mary by the Holy Spirit.

In fact on this the feast day we hear the passage in the gospel of Luke describing the archangel Gabriel coming to Mary and he tells her that she will become pregnant by the power of the most high overshadowing her. Pretty easy to be confused.

But no that is not what we celebrate today. We celebrate the conception of Mary. This feast was created by Pope Pius IX in 1854 and it became dogma which is defined as "a truth revealed by God, which the magisterium of the Church declared as binding."

Clearly our blessed virgin Mary is a special person. God called her she said yes and Jesus was born. Not sure how many of us would be willing to walk in her shoes and that is why the Pope declared she is that special that she must have had an Immaculate Conception to do what she did. And thank God for that, thank God for Mary!

So all that is clearly awesome but what I would like to call your attention to today is what St Paul says in our second reading from Ephesians. He says "Blessed be the God and Father of our Lord Jesus, who has **blessed us in Christ** with very spiritual blessing in the heavens, as **he has chose us in him** before the foundation of the world to be holy and without blemish before him."

Wow. God chose us in Christ before the foundation of the world.?. Paul isn't talking about Mary he's talking about us! Like Mary we too have been chosen and called by God. Not to give birth to Gods son but to allow others to be born spiritually through Gods invitation through our words and actions.

Everyone is called by God. God wants everyone to know him and to be with him. We have been chosen to help God bring that about here.

Will we have the courage like our blessed virgin mother to say yes? That is what we really celebrate today. That through Marys conception and the birth of Jesus we have come to know God, to know he loves us and that we have been chosen to do the same. Let's get out there and get the job done!

This space is for you to record your comments or your groups comments

THIRD SUNDAY OF ADVENT - YEAR A

Is 35:1-6a,10; Ps 146; James 5:7-10; Matt 11:2-11

Jesus asks the crowd in our gospel from Matthew today about John the Baptist, "What did you go to the desert to see? A reed swayed by the wind?.. Someone dressed in fine clothing?"

He then asks "why did you go see him? To see a prophet?" He goes on to say "yes.. John is a prophet the one whom it is written "Behold I am sending my messenger ahead of you; he will prepare your way before you."

That quote that Matthew attributed to Jesus is from Malachi 3:1. A few lines down in verse 23 Malachi says he will send Elijah the prophet so it's an interesting reference. A priest I know said that Jesus is saying that John the Baptist is the second coming of Elijah. Further down in Matthew in 17 a conversation between the disciples and Jesus takes place in regards to this. So if you'd like to go deeper on that check it out!

Today though, I would like to look at the questions that Jesus asks the crowd. What did you expect to see? Why did you go to the desert?

I was asking myself these questions in the context of what do I expect to see when I come to Mass and Why do I go to Mass? Or why do I go to the desert of prayer perhaps?

First what I expect and hope to see when I go to Mass is a full church. A parish family eager to pray for each other and receive Jesus body and blood in the Eucharist. The food to strengthen us for the journey.

As far as why because I need the nourishment the encouragement of the parish's prayers for me and the strength that the Eucharist gives me. That's really all it is for me. We need to have a public prayer life which should manifest itself in attending Mass with the community and private prayer in quiet with God.

That private prayer is a desert we go to get away from the noise and hectic life we lead and to spend quality time talking with God. Both prayer types help us to prepare for Christmas and whatever everyday has to throw at us.

Thank God for John the Baptist who gives us the example like Jesus in the garden of retiring to a quiet place to talk with God. If we are not already doing so let's try and retreat even for just 10 minutes to the desert of quiet prayer and reflect on and ask God for guidance and to help us recognize his presence in the sacraments and everyone we meet each day.

This space is for you to record your comments or your groups comments

FOURTH SUNDAY OF ADVENT - YEAR A

Is 7:10-14; Ps 24; Rom 1:1-7; Mt 1:18-24

Matthew's gospel today introduces us to Joseph - "a righteous man" who was betrothed to Mary. Joseph learns that his fiancé is pregnant and decides to not expose her to the law publicly because that would have led her to death.

Think about his initial disappointment and all the thought's running through his head. The pain of learning that apparently Mary had been unfaithful to him.

Then, while asleep the Lord tells him through an angel in a dream "Joseph son of David do not be afraid to take Mary as your wife .. for it is through the Holy Spirit that this child has been conceived .. you are to name him Jesus because he will save his people from their sins."

Ok Lord can do! ☺ I have reflected on this passage many times and I always think could I have had the faith and courage that Joseph had to answer the call from God? How did he really know it was God? How long did he discern the message before acting?

And what about Mary? Think about her sitting at her parents house waiting and wondering what will happen to her.?. She said yes to God's angel Gabriel, she knew that God was working but how was this going to work with Joseph? Guessing a little stressful for the Blessed Mother.

Maybe sometimes we think too much. We try to control things, happenings. We know what we want and so we plan and do what we need to do so things come out "right", which is to say we get what we want.

But then God has a different plan for us. Things happen and all of a sudden our plans are either not attainable or simply not possible.

I think the message from Joseph today is that we need to listen to God. We need to take it one day at a time. Live in the present moment where God is indeed present to us.

The plans we make may not be what God wants for us. Somehow like Mary too we need to just wait to see what will happen all the while trusting in Him who loves us more than we can ever know and wants us to be filled with happiness and joy.

It may not look or feel that way at this very moment. You may be going through something terrible. God hasn't done this to you, no he is suffering with you. Somehow he will get you through the suffering and you will have peace again. No idea how but we must not loose faith; He will bring us closer to him and deliver us from the trouble.

As Paul tells us in the second reading, we have been called like Joseph and Mary to bring about, "the obedience of faith for the sake of his name". We will receive "grace and peace from God our father and the Lord Jesus Christ." Come Lord Jesus!

This space is for you to record your comments or your groups comments

THE NATIVITY OF THE LORD - MASS DURING THE DAY YEAR A

Is 52:7-10; Ps 98; Heb 1:1-6; John 1:1-18

Not sure about you but I was expecting the gospel to be describing the scene in Bethlehem that we are all so familiar with. The barn with the baby Jesus in the manger, Mary leaning over keeping an eye on him and of course Joseph. Sprinkle in some animals, maybe a shepherd or two. The wise men of course come next week during Epiphany.

Nope none of that. We hear the very beginning of John's gospel. John doesn't have a nativity narrative like Matthew and Luke.

Instead he begins at the very beginning. John talks about the Word of God - who of course is the Christ, Jesus - John says the Word was there at the beginning of creation and "all things came to be through him… What came to be through him was life."

It's important for us to realize that God the Trinity is not sequential. Often we think we have God the Father, then the Son and then the Holy Spirit comes and is given to us. No they were all three present at the beginning as we say in the creed - "begotten not made consubstantial with the Father."

In our second reading from Hebrews the author talks about how God speaks to us through his Son and that he "is the refulgence - which means the quality of being bright and sending out rays - of his glory, the very imprint of his being". The very life of his being.

So God came to us through Jesus to show us that He is with us. As Jesus grows and begins his ministry He shows us the power and the mercy of God through his healing and miracles and teaches us to be selfless like him.

That is what we take comfort in and celebrate today and every Sunday for that matter. That Jesus Christ, the Son of God was born and has taught us how to live unselfishly and through his way we will find the peace and joy that we seek.

Thank you Jesus Christ, thank you God the Father and Holy Spirit for revealing yourself to us in the Nativity and then in the ministry of Jesus, in the ministry of the Apostles and the ministry of your Church. Help us to recognize your presence in the sacraments and all living things here on earth. That we may serve them as you intend us to and enjoy your great mercy at the end of our lives in the full presence in heaven.

Merry Christmas!!

This space is for you to record your comments or your groups comments

SOLEMNITY OF MARY, THE HOLY MOTHER OF GOD - YEAR A

Num 6:22-27; Ps 67; Gal 4:4-7; Lk 2:16-21

In our Gospel from Luke today we have Mary the Holy Mother of God and her husband Joseph with their baby lying in a manger. In Luke, shepherds rather than the Magi/Three Wise Men come to pay him homage. These shepherds were out in the field just outside of Bethlehem and the reading said they went in haste to see the baby when they heard of his birth.

The shepherds returned to their sheep and told everyone they met about the baby. Mary for her part and Joseph for his did what the angel commanded they named the baby Jesus.

Pauls letter to the Galatians also confirms for us the human birth of Jesus and adds that God also sent his Spirit into our hearts that we now would become brothers in Christ, heirs of heaven through God's grace.

All of this because Mary said yes let it be done to me. We are truly blessed and God shows his mercy to us thanks to Mary. Let us turn to God and listen to see where he wants us to say Yes so that more can come to recognize Jesus the son of God and learn through his many teachings each week of this new year. Let us go like the shepherds and tell everyone we meet about this Jesus!

This space is for you to record your comments or your groups comments

SOLEMNITY OF THE EPIPHANY OF THE LORD - YEAR A

Is 60:1-6; Ps 72; Eph 3:2-3a,5-6; Mt 2:1-12

In Poland the feast of the Epiphany or as they call it the "feast of the three kings" is celebrated on the designated day which is January 6th. All businesses are closed, no banking it is a holiday just like Christmas is to us on December 25th.

I happened to be in Poland on the feast day many years ago at a friends home and the parish priest along with altar servers visited the home for a few minutes offering a blessing to everyone present and then on a door frame with chalk he wrote the names of the three kings. It was very special tradition one that would be very difficult to do here in the US.

Also, some other countries call Epiphany "Little Christmas" and families will actually exchange gifts on this day rather than Christmas as they mimic the gift giving of the Magi of Gold, Frankincense and myrrh.

So why is this such a special day for us? For one I think Matthew is trying to show that Jesus has been born not just for Jews but for all mankind. The Wise Men are from the East most likely present day Iran and they are inspired by God through their religious interpretation via the stars to pack up everything and follow the star which would end up taking them to Bethlehem.

St Paul in the second reading from Ephesians echoes that this Jesus is far more than a Jewish king he is to bring the presence of God to the Gentiles, all non Jewish people and that they too will share in his kingdom and become copartners in the promise of Christ.

So this is truly good news! We are all part of who Jesus came to teach, heal, and save. We too are special and we will learn that He - God - loves us and wants to have a relationship with us.

The relationship starts easy enough by coming to know a baby and his parents. But as the year progresses our relationship needs to mature as we together with the baby grow and age our spiritual life needs to grow and age too. This Jesus is going to start changing the way we think which should in turn change the way we act. This is what the word repentance really means changing one's mind!

Today it begins. We've come to pay the baby homage along with the three kings from the East. We will never know exactly what they did other than they went home via a different route because in a dream they were told not to go back to Herod as he had wished. Clearly Herod was jealous and wanted to do the baby harm.

But did their lives change after seeing the baby? We don't really know all we know is they left. What are we going to do? Are we going to leave too? Or are we going to stay with Jesus and mature with him body and soul?

Next week we will be fast forwarding to Jesus being baptized by John and his mission to bring God into the world will start in earnest. Are we ready? It's fun and easy to hang with the baby Jesus but the adult Jesus is going to challenge us to do more than just hang with him. Let us take to prayer our intention to grow with Jesus and to help Jesus bring his kingdom and love to all we encounter. May he give us the grace to do this effectively.

This space is for you to record your comments or your groups comments

FIRST SUNDAY OF ADVENT - YEAR B

Is 63:16b-17,19b;64:2-7, Ps 80, 1Cor 1:3-9, Mark 13:33-37

Watch! You do not know when the lord of the house is coming. He could come at anytime and you must he ready. Be ready for what? Ready to be judged guilty? Clearly we are all guilty of sin. Nothing we can do on our own can fix that.

Paul thankfully comes through and says to us don't worry! For the grace of God bestowed on you in Christ Jesus, that in him you were enriched in every way.... You are not lacking in any spiritual gift as you wait - watch - for the revelation of our Lord Jesus Christ.

Paul continues God is faithful and by him you were called to fellowship with his son Jesus Christ our Lord. Hallelujah thanks be to God! It isn't up to us. We can't screw this is up because God loves us. We need not be fearful. Thank you God, Thank you Paul.

Now we can watch and wait with joy and anticipation like we watch the clock as we wait to go on vacation. We can get excited about Jesus coming back. How awesome it will be to praise him and worship him and thank him for his love and mercy.

This story isn't about us seeking perfection. When we do that we start to think hey look at me I'm doing pretty good. I'm earning this salvation

I deserve this because I have done all this stuff right and that person over there doesn't have it right and he's going to be in big trouble when Jesus comes.

If that is how we read the gospel then we don't know Jesus. Our desire to love and be holy starts with Jesus within us. His grace moves us to be better and more loving and more Christ like. It is not us. Sure we need to be open to it and recognize the grace but it all starts with him.

Thank God "our father" as we hear Isaiah call him a long time before the Lord pulled those words into our favorite prayer. Clearly the Lord was acknowledging that God graced Isaiah with that beautiful imagery of God as loving father and gives it to us as our most important prayer.

Unfortunately Isaiah didn't have the benefit of knowing Jesus the Christ. He did not yet understand that God wasn't angry because we have sinned but that God would show us His love through his son Jesus to help us understand that He is not angry.

A love that is unlike any love that we could understand. A love that doesn't get angry but a love that heals and bring everlasting love and joy. Of course Isaiah knows this now.

We too will know this for certain one day. So keep watching, get excited, anticipate, tell your friends! Perhaps your friends aren't here with us today. Maybe they heard a sermon that said God is angry because of their sin and we're turned off. I think when people know people that are more loving than God is depicted to them they move away from God and I think that is natural. We need to tell them that is not how God is. We need to tell them that God loves them and is not coming to punish them but to bring them back into his love and the joy that comes with it. Our Father who art in heaven loves you very much.

Come watch for the Lord for He is coming soon! He wants to show you the love he has for you. Don't forget to tell your friends to come and wait and watch with us!

This space is for you to record your comments or your groups comments

SECOND SUNDAY OF ADVENT - YEAR B

Is 40:1-5,9-11; Ps85; Peter 3:8-14; Mark 1:1-8

"For the Lord one day is like a thousand years and a thousand years like one day" we hear in Peter's second letter. The concept of time is of this creation. The earth spins on its axis each day and revolves around the sun each year. Though we have seen it in the movies we can't go back in time to "back to the future" as the movie was named but to God it is all one time space.

Jesus's apostles and disciples thought he would be returning quickly certainly within their lifetime. And when he didn't the people started to get restless. Peter is trying to assure them that this could take some time. Jesus will be back when the time is right.

They say our mind has a tough time understanding eternity, infinity. If we try to think about God and time I think about it as Him standing in front of a table with a big piece of plywood on it and he sees all of eternity from left to right.

He can see the "time" when we were born he sees the time when we are to die, he sees when Jesus was born and he sees when Jesus dies and is resurrected. He also sees all of the Masses that have occurred across time all happening in the same God time space.

That is why Mass is like traveling back in time for us. When the priest does the consecration of the bread and wine for us He is United with Jesus saying the same words to his apostles at the same time. Our Eucharist is the same Eucharist that the apostles shared. God sees both events happening side by side in real time. That is just amazing to think about.

John the Baptist tells the people of Israel today in the gospel that the Messiah the Christ is coming soon. Repent from sin, get baptized and commit to sin no more. One mightier than him is coming who will baptize you with the Holy Spirit.

As we look at Gods piece of plywood we see John right there announcing this. And we see indeed Jesus here baptizing the apostles with the Holy Spirit and we see our baptism and our confirmation right there too.

And yes if we look to the right we see Jesus coming in glory. The message today is we shouldn't wait for that. We can experience the Kingdom of God today and now. Jesus has given us the tools and the direction of what we need to do this.

It is for us to focus on becoming more like him. Becoming selfless and serve others. In other words clear the sin out of your life, repent as John the Baptist talks about. Sin is simply selfishness. It's putting our own needs in front of others and often times hurting people and relationships when we do that.

The good news is God is watching us on the big board. Not with a frown or being disgusted but with a little loving smile and do you know why?

As he looks to the right on his board he sees you trying to do better and he sees your belief, your faith and hope that you have because Jesus Christ came into the world on Christmas and you received the Holy Spirit and you are ready to help Jesus bring about his kingdom not at the end of time but right here now. Let's do it!

This space is for you to record your comments or your groups comments

THIRD SUNDAY OF ADVENT - YEAR B

Is 61:1-2a, 10-11; Psalm (Lk1); Thes 5:16-24; John 1:6-8,19-28

Paul tells us today to "Rejoice always. Pray without ceasing. In all circumstances give thanks, for this is the will of God for you in Christ Jesus."

Well in 2020 that has been tough to follow. I certainly have not been rejoicing and if this is Gods will for me why in the world should I be rejoicing?

Suffering is a tough thing to understand. It is the mystery of the cross that somehow at sometime we will all suffer like Jesus. Maybe that has been you this year or right now. Maybe not. Maybe all is good with you right now but perhaps you have journeyed through suffering maybe last year and it's a little better for you now.

Whatever the case we will all suffer. Jesus shows us how to do it by surrendering it and offering it up in prayer to him, to God. When we suffer, when we can't control what is happening to us either physically or emotionally we can't fix it. If we could we would but we can't. Our only recourse is to pray and offer it to God to Jesus to fix it, to take us through this pain.

Eventually he will. Eventually in Gods time you will be healed if He has more things for you to do for Him here or you will resurrect and enter His presence and then you will certainly rejoice always.

Let's talk about the pray unceasing part. I don't believe Paul is asking you to sit and say the Rosary every minute of every day, that is not his point. His point is we must recognize Gods presence within our soul each minute. That every beat of our heart is a prayer or it should be seen that way. It may be a prayer for help and healing, it may be a prayer consolation for a friend it must be a prayer of thanksgiving in recognition of his presence in our lives in our soul.

For that is what we celebrate in 2 weeks with Christmas. Gods incarnation in Jesus Christ and the fact that God is incarnate in all his creation in all living things especially in us.

We should not fear our God for He loves us more than we can understand. He wants us to experience and recognize his presence in our lives. He doesn't want you to be afraid of him. He wants your "Soul to rejoice in him". We need to recognize that "the Spirit of the Lord God is upon you and me because he has anointed us" in Baptism and Confirmation.

The next sentence is key in the Isaiah's reading today. "He has sent me to bring glad tidings to the poor to heal the broken hearted to proclaim liberty and set the captives free". We don't do these things because if we don't God will condemn us, no. We do those things because we love God and recognize him in our midst and though we may be suffering we have hope in him. For it is God that actually inspires us to do all the good that we do that way we don't have to worry about taking credit for the idea. Grace has moved us.

When we do help others who are hurting we receive joy and peace. Like John the Baptist we point to Jesus as the reason for our joy our perseverance in suffering our hope and our salvation.

Today on this Third Sunday of Advent let us "rejoice heartily in the Lord our God for in my God is the joy of my soul."

This space is for you to record your comments or your groups comments

FOURTH SUNDAY OF ADVENT - YEAR B

Sam 7:1-5,8b-12,14a,16; Ps 89; Rom 16:25-27; Lk 1:26-38

If you have grown up Catholic and perhaps even if you didn't you are most likely familiar with this gospel reading from Luke today. Gabriel the archangel visits Mary and tells her she is going to become pregnant and have a baby and he will sit on the throne of David and his kingdom will have no end.

Our beloved prayer the Hail Mary comes from this passage. "Hail Mary full of grace the Lord is with you!" This the Annunciation of the Lord is one of the Joyful mysteries that we ponder when saying the Rosary on Mondays and Thursdays during the year and on Sundays from Advent until Lent.

This passage and especially the last sentence is also part of a regular Catholic prayer often said at noon time everyday called the Angelus - "Behold I am the handmade of the Lord be it done to me according to your word." The Angelus prayer starts with "The angel of the Lord declared unto Mary and she conceived of the Holy Spirit".

The Church in her wisdom asks us to ponder this passage in prayer everyday at noon and in our regular recitation of the Rosary. Why do you think that is? There are so many things we can take from this for our own lives.

We see Mary first recognizing God in her life through prayer and the message of an angel. We see her saying yes to God and trusting God even though this decision will bring her hardship and pain and maybe even divorce and stoning to be pregnant when not married was a serious thing and most woman were sentenced to death. Talk about faith and trusting God!

I am guessing we might have trouble trusting God as much as Mary did. I know I would. The truth is I struggle to be selfless. I struggle to give up my will. Even though I say "your will be done" several times a day I still really want my will to be done.

Thankfully God knows this and loves me anyway and loves you too. He continues to send his messengers, his angels to us each day to call us to service in his name. We will hear them when we are in quiet prayer and contemplation. Just listening. He calls us to help our friends to know him and to find peace and joy amongst their suffering.

Becoming more selfless, more Christ like is a process, a journey. It doesn't end with our declaration of faith in him as our savior, no it will be a life long commitment of saying yes to him everyday and doing and making the right decisions, the selfless decisions, the decisions to love like He did, like he still does today through those who follow him.

Today as we go to prayer let us take to heart and make the words of Mary our own - "Behold, I am the handmade of the Lord. May it be done to me according to your word." Then ponder what He is looking for you to do in His name this day. What selfless act is in front of you to do? Listen and you will find out.

This space is for you to record your comments or your groups comments

THE NATIVITY OF THE LORD - YEAR B

Is 52:7-10; Ps98; Heb1:1-6; John 1:1-18

As I was trying to figure out what to write on Christmas, I poured through all the readings for Christmas Eve, Mass at Night, Christmas Day Mass at Dawn and during the Day. I settled in on the readings from the Mass during the day.

Two of the selected readings are the beginning of the books - Hebrews the second reading and the gospel of John. I really like the beginning of John because he sets things straight right for us at the beginning.

"In the beginning was the Word, and the Word was with God, and the Word was God. He was in the beginning with God. All things came to be through him, through him was life."

So now we understand how he heals and controls the elements. Jesus is God, it's that simple really. As Hebrews said "for to which angels did God ever say "You are my son". Isaiah cries out to us "Your God is King!"

What's great about these readings especially the Gospel it helps us to realize the three persons of God - The Trinity- was not at all sequential. It wasn't just God the Father at creation then when creation messed up he sent Jesus and then when Jesus died, resurrected and ascended into heaven, He gave us the Holy Spirit. No not at all. All three were present during creation. All three were present in the incarnation of Jesus in the manger and all three are present to us in the sacraments, in each of us in all the living things in creation.

It's always been this way. Man designates beautiful churches like ours as holy places but all places are holy because God made them and God is present there. See we have trouble with understanding this infinite, eternal God. We have trouble understanding the abundance of love poured out everyday for us from God in the love of family, friends and strangers.

Our Psalm rightly says "all the ends of the earth have seen the saving power of God". That's because He is present to all the ends of the earth and always has been.

It's important to realize Jesus wasn't plan B. The Trinity is not sequential. Jesus wasn't the clean up crew. No Jesus was plan A. God always intended to manifest himself in creation to show us that He is with us and loves us and will never leave us. We commemorate this incarnation of Jesus Christ today and we know Jesus points to the reality of God's presence everywhere - His presence in the world.

Now knowing that His presence is in us we have a responsibility to be His loving presence to others. To make known this joyful news to all we encounter that Christ is born today! God is with us!

This space is for you to record your comments or your groups comments

FEAST OF THE HOLY FAMILY - YEAR B

Sir 3:2-6; Ps128; Col 3:12-21; Luke 2:22-40

In modern time I suspect preachers tend not to like the second reading from Paul's letter to the Colossians. You can see in the missal that there are even brackets around the text that says "Wives be subordinate to your husbands as is proper in the Lord." Some translations even use the word submissive which seems even more harsh.

According to Paul all husbands need to do is love their wives and avoid bitterness to them. Seems simple enough to love someone. But is it? When you truly love someone you will do anything for that person. The greatest love is shown when one lays down his life for another we hear elsewhere in scripture. When in love you give up your will to do the will of others.

Is that not what family life is about? We grow up, all of us, sons, daughters, mothers, fathers, uncles,aunts, grandparents learning how to love how to be selfless. That learning doesn't stop when we leave our parents home no if we are doing it right we continue to learn until we die.

This love training is preparing us for the ultimate love at our death. When we will truly give up our will or ego and transform and recognize our true self which is his presence in us. That my friends is resurrection. Some of us will hold on to that will and ego right through death going kicking and screaming as they say.

But God doesn't give up on us, his family. We don't miss the boat if we haven't got there yet. Purgatory is God loving us even when we don't deserve it because there are very few of us that figure this out before they die. We call them the Saints. But God will make us all Saints one day.

When we see Him and we see all the family members who have passed before us waiting to greet us after Jesus, our ego and will melts to the floor and we are purified by a loving embrace by Jesus.

Family life as we know it here is part of the preparation. Work at it. As Paul says show kindness, compassion, humility, patience, forgiveness. For this is what God will do with us. Love is eternal. Your family is eternal. We will be together forever in Gods love.

This space is for you to record your comments or your groups comments

MARY THE MOTHER OF GOD - YEAR B

Num 6:22-27; Ps67;Ga 4:4-7;Lk 2:16-21

If I remember right the blessing proclaimed in the reading from Numbers today became the basis for an Irish blessing. "The Lord bless you and keep you. The Lord let his face shine upon you and be gracious to you. The Lord look upon you kindly and give you peace."

Mary and Joseph would have been very familiar with this passage this prayer. I am sure this along with the prayer and the angels of course got them through some rather tough times in the early going of family life. Think about all that has happened in the nine months.

Mary is pregnant through the Holy Spirit, Joseph has to figure out if this is true or is he being duped a fool. But the angels direct him to do the right thing. Then the census is called and they have to up and leave home to go to Bethlehem because Joseph is of the house of David and that is their home town.

Of course they get there and there is no room at the Inn so they camp out in a stable and it is there that Jesus is born. Their perseverance is remarkable. They just keep pushing the ball forward. One day at a time.

As they sit there one day the shepherds arrive and tell them the angles have spoken to them and that they must come and see the child for he will be king. So they do. Mary kept all these things in her heart along with all the other happenings and she simply realizes this is Gods will. This is what is supposed to be happening to me right now this is my purpose. To raise this son who will one day be a great king.

What is happening in your life? What are you asking God to help you with? What are you persevering through? Let us take the example of Mary and Joseph and trust the Lord and lay it at his altar and simply say I believe and I am here to do your will. Help me to recognize you and do what you wish. Shine your face upon me and give me peace.

This space is for you to record your comments or your groups comments

THE EPIPHANY OF
THE LORD - YEAR B

IS 60:1-6; Ps 72; Eph 3:2-3a, 5-6; Matt 2:1-12

The Few, The Proud, The Marines! How many of you are Marines? Thank you for your service. Other branches of the service? Thank you.

Few people over the course of the centuries recognized God's presence in the world, in creation. The three guys we hear about today, the Few, the proud the Magi certainly did. For they heard Gods whisper to them and saw God had placed a star in the sky for them to follow.

These guys weren't Israelites or Jews they were gentiles from the East yet God spoke to them and God manifested himself to them that they might lead others to recognize God and come to know God and come to love God. I have always looked at the story and reflected on how God can manifest himself in different ways to different people. We sometimes like to put God in a box, our box but that makes God pretty small. We need to be open to the reality of Gods presence in the world and his creation everywhere.

Clearly the prophets that recognized God in antiquity were few in number too. But they tried to tell the Israelites about God's abundant love and mercy but, Nope, no thanks not many got it.

But the Trinitarian God had a plan. He would send himself incarnated as human to call more to him and so Jesus the Christ was born and was indeed recognized by the Magi and the shepherds of Bethlehem. As Jesus grows and becomes an adult he calls more and more but still in comparison to the total number of people on this earth it is still just a few that recognize God in their lives.

Even with Paul hearing and acting on the stewardship of God's grace for our benefit we still struggle to believe and recognize Emmanuel - God is with us. I think we make belief to transactional. We do this so we can get something yet as Paul so often tells us it is not what we do but it is Gods grace that initiates all that is good gives us hope and peace. It's not the worthiness game that does, we don't earn that hope and peace.

And you know it is Ok for us to fill up this church with people. We want many many more to believe right? Even if that means one Sunday you might not get "your seat" because a stranger is sitting there. How great would that be? Not great at all for where am I to sit? We don't like taking turns or sharing, I think we actually like the Few the Proud the Mass goers. We don't like change and we don't like people that are undeserving to be sitting in our seat.

Well news flash no one is deserving of the Grace of God and don't worry there is plenty of Grace to go around! The more people that come to worship and recognize God the more grace is given to this world and it just keeps on going like that. More come, more grace, more peace.

So us few need to help others come to know the peace of knowing God. We can't hide it just for ourselves. We can't save our seat. We must love God and give away our riches that God bestowed on us in the first place.

Come let us worship and love God and take that love into the world so many, many more will come to know him and we will finally have peace on earth.

This space is for you to record your comments or your groups comments

THE BAPTISM OF
THE LORD - YEAR B

Is 42:1-4,6-7; Psalm – 29; 1John 5:1-9: Mark 1:7-11

For many I am sure you don't remember your baptism. You were babies and with the exception of some pictures and stories about how cute you were that is all you know.

If you were baptized when you were older I am sure you remember. You remember saying Yes to Jesus and his church. Yes Lord I believe that you are son of God and Son of Mary.

Us cradle Catholics did get the chance to proclaim that ourselves of course at our Confirmation. I am sure most all of you can at least remember some of that day especially if the Bishop was able to be present.

It is a big deal - Confirmation - that's why the ordinary minister of Confirmation is the Bishop. When the Bishop dips his thumb in the Chrism oil and makes the sign of the cross on your forehead and says "be sealed with the gift of the Holy Spirit" and your response is Amen and then places his hand on the top of your head "Peace be with you" and we respond "and with your spirit."

We are confirming the presence of the Holy Spirit, the presence of the Trinitarian God in our lives that was first recognized by our parents and

God parents at our Baptism. We further commit to sharing that spirit that God with others through service.

We hear in Mark today that a voice from heaven was heard when Jesus came out of the Jordan after John baptized him that said "You are my beloved son; with you I am well pleased".

These words are a direct quote from Isaiah in our first reading. The Old Testament will be fulfilled in the next 2 years of Jesus ministry which began officially with his baptism by John the Baptist.

Another John, the apostle John "the one whom Jesus loved" says to us in the second reading right at the beginning "everyone who believes that Jesus is the Christ is begotten by God". What does begotten mean? Merriam Webster says it means "brought into existence by or as if by a parent" hence we believe that Jesus is the son of God, part of the Trinity.

But John is saying if we believe then we too are begotten by God. He goes on to say that to love God is to keep his commandments and those commandments are not burdensome for those begotten by God and further whoever is begotten by God conquers the world and the victory that conquers the world is our faith.

The faith that we said yes to at our Baptism and our Confirmation. Today we not only celebrate the Lords baptism we celebrate our own initiation into the church into our faith. We believe that Jesus is begotten by God and so are we. Later in the gospel we hear that Jesus will pray to God the Father that we recognize His presence - their presence in our lives. Once we do that the burdens will be less.

We can lean on the strength that is the presence of God, the Holy Spirit that is within us will help us persevere. And finally on our final day here on earth, when we get to heaven we too will hear God say to us "You are my beloved Child with you I am well pleased. Come and be with me forever."

This space is for you to record your comments or your groups comments

FIRST SUNDAY OF ADVENT - YEAR C

Jer 33:14-16; Ps 25; Thess 3:12-4:2; Lk 21:25-28, 34-36

In Luke's gospel today, this first day of the new liturgical year, we hear Jesus himself talking about his return to earth after his death and resurrection.

After talking about the signs and people dying of fright from those signs, Jesus proclaims "They will see the Son of Man coming in a cloud with power and great glory. But when these signs begin to happen, stand erect and raise your hands because your redemption is at hand."

In other words, don't be afraid! Don't die of fright, don't cower in the corner or hide under a table! Stand erect and raise your hands!

We are comfortable doing that because we follow Paul's advice in the second reading to continually increase our love for one another just as Paul had done for them. By loving our neighbors we become part of the saving works of Christ. We are his hands and feet here to help the poor and forgotten, here to feed the thousands of people starving both with food and the saving food the Word of God, the good news that Jesus came and is coming again.

Let us take the encouragement given to us today and "lift our souls up to the Lord" as the Psalm says so that he will guide us in truth and teach us what he needs us to do for him today and everyday.

Don't be afraid of Jesus's second coming but instead welcome it and expect it everyday. Prepare with daily prayer and recognize his presence already incarnate in creation. May our prayer make us humble Lord to do your justice. "For all the paths of the Lord are kindness and constancy toward those who keep his covenant" of love.

This space is for you to record your comments or your groups comments

SECOND SUNDAY OF ADVENT - YEAR C

Bar 5:1-9; Ps 126; Phil 1:4-6, 8-11; Lk 3:1-6

As a kid I always loved Advent. It was my favorite time of the year. I loved seeing the wreath each week in church as we lit one candle and then another. The anticipation of knowing once we get all the candles lit the next Mass is Christmas! That of course meant Santa and gifts under the tree.

In the readings today there is great anticipation too. John the Baptist is "a voice crying out in the desert: prepare the way of the Lord" get ready turn from your broken and sinful ways. Many believe John and they receive a baptism in the Jordan and go on trying to live better lives so that when the Lord comes He will find them living with purpose and in love.

Paul in the second reading after telling the Philippians how much he is praying for them to continue the good work they have started, tells them that his prayer is that the love, the goodness that they are doing in community increases more and more to discern what is of value.

The world we live in values things and money. But the world Jesus wants and John the Baptist and Paul talk about is a world focused on selfless love and community. The game of Life is not a game where at the end, the people with the most toys win. As we see on the news truly those with the most toys usually loose their way and are not happy. And we know of course that everything we have is a grace a gift from God.

The point today is we need to keep trying to improve to become more self-less. As Baruch describes we need to take off our robes of mourning and misery and put in the splendor of glory from God forever. We cannot be afraid to share our faith with others. Though we will most likely be scorned we must persevere in the hope that those family members or friends or neighbors will realize that what we do each week gives us a peace, a joy and a happiness that the world cannot provide.

Our work is never done. The keyword in Baruch is forever. We must love forever we must be generous forever we must honor God forever and continue to make straight the path so that when he comes at the end of time or we go to him at the end of our time we can surrender ourselves to him knowing we have done our best to further his kingdom and He will bring us into His eternal rest with the faithful departed. For "The Lord has done great things for us; we are filled with joy."

This space is for you to record your comments or your groups comments

THIRD SUNDAY OF ADVENT - YEAR C

Zeph 3:14-18a; Ps (IS 12); Philippians 4:4-7; Luke 3:10-18

What should we do? That is the question the people asked John the Baptist and it should be the question we are asking during Advent. How should we prepare for Christmas what should we do?

John tells everyone basically share what you have with the less fortunate. Give your extra coat, give your extra food. We don't do this because it's nice or what we should do we do it because it is God who has provided our cloak and our food to us in the first place.

Paul tells us this indirectly and suggests we praise God with worship thanksgiving and ultimately through rejoicing! By recognizing God's grace in our life and realizing it is not the worthiness game that we have earned all the stuff we have and such that those without just need to work as hard as us! Not!

Once we accept this truth we will know "the peace of God that surpasses all understanding will guard your hearts and minds in Christ Jesus." Rejoice! Again I say Rejoice! The Lord is near!

This space is for you to record your comments or your groups comments

FOURTH SUNDAY OF ADVENT - YEAR C

Mic 5:1-4a; Ps 80; Heb 10:5-10; Lk 1:39-45

All the candles are lit. It is the fourth Sunday of Advent. Todays gospel from Luke tells the story of the Visitation of the Blessed Virgin Mary when she goes to see her cousin Elizabeth who is pregnant with John the Baptist.

Clearly our Hail Mary prayer comes from these words of Elizabeth. "Blessed are you among women and blessed is the fruit of your womb". And though the last sentence isn't in our prayer it is still pretty important- "Blessed are you who believed that what was spoken to you by the Lord would be fulfilled."

Elizabeth is referring back to the Annunciation when the angel Gabriel visits Mary to tell her that she will bear a son by the Holy Spirit. Her obedience to do Gods will is unmatched with the exception of Jesus accepting the cross so that we might come to know Gods love for us through His suffering and our suffering.

In the second reading from the letter to the Hebrews the author reminds his listeners that the Christ told them that sin offerings and the animal sacrifices was not what God intended. Those acts led the people to the worthiness game. If I do this and you don't I'm better than you. No the answer is to do Gods will like Jesus does on the cross.

We too must do His will. He has put us here for a reason. Something only we are designated to do. We will suffer too, it will not be easy. But if we surrender the difficulty to the Lord and persevere we will find Joy.

As we close in on the celebration of the nativity let us turn to God and thank him for our blessings, thank him for his presence and incarnation in Jesus Christ and in all of his magnificent creation. And finally let us humbly turn to him in prayer and offer all that is troubling us on this altar today so that he may give us new life and save us. Come Lord Jesus!

This space is for you to record your comments or your groups comments

VIGIL MASS - THE NATIVITY OF OUR LORD JESUS CHRIST - YEAR C

Is 62:1-5; Ps 89; Acts 13:16-17,22-25;Matt 1:1-25

As the prophet said, "Behold the virgin shall conceive and bear a son, and they shall name him Emmanuel which means God is with us." God is with us! He is here not only incarnate in Jesus Christ but in us and all living things.

Christianity is the only religion to believe of this presence of God within creation. We recognize the Christ presence in our sacraments, our relationships with family and friends, in the trees of the forests the animals all of creation as St Francis reminds us so often in his works.

Do we believe this? We are here tonight so I guess on some level we at least want to believe this. But if we truly believed we would do things differently wouldn't we? Would we yell and scream at people on the highway who cut us off, would we gossip about a person we know who trusts us as a friend, would we hoard our food and collect so much stuff?

I don't think so. Tonight as we gaze upon the lowly stable that Jesus was born in and contemplate the poverty in which he entered this world can we think about all those living in a stable tonight? Can we think about those going hungry tonight?

What can we do about it Armand? I don't know what you can do but we have to do something. God is with us he is in us and He wants us to do something! He wants everyone to feel the joy of Christmas that you will feel when you go home tonight.

And I know and understand for some here tonight there may not be joy. Many of us have lost loved ones this past year and that weighs heavy on our hearts as it should. The first Christmas without a loved one. But we are people of hope. We know that those deceased loved ones are with us too, present to us here and everywhere through the Holy Spirit. Can you feel them close by? If not try sitting in silence and I am sure you will be warmed by their presence.

No matter what is going on in our lives Christmas and the Lord always comes to us everyday. I pray that this Christmas you truly recognize his presence and help him and his church spread his good news, the message of the gospel. For ever I will sing the goodness of the Lord! Merry Christmas!

This space is for you to record your comments or your groups comments

THE HOLY FAMILY
OF JESUS, MARY, AND
JOSEPH - YEAR C

Sam 1:20-22,24-28; Ps 84; 1John 3:1-2, 21-24; Lk 2:41-52

Can you imagine losing your child for four days? Not knowing where he is? I remember being at Disney World and my 5 year old son walked away from us. It was the longest ten minutes of my life I can't imagine Four days.

Parents primary job is to keep their children safe. To provide for them physically with food and clothing, shelter from the elements and from the evil that lurks around us.

As the kids advance in age and wisdom they begin to ask questions. Why? As in why we're you looking for me? What? None of my friends have to do that! Where? I don't want to go there!

Those conversations can certainly cause tension and stress. Parents just want to keep their kids safe and kids as they grow just want to start taking care of themselves.

If we admit it as young kids maybe 5 or 6 our parents are awesome, the best! When we get to 12 or 14 somehow our parents have become imbeciles. They know nothing. Then somewhere around graduation from high school or college and we get our first real job and have been at it a bit we realize - wow. My parents have been doing this for 20 years?!? And with that realization we go back to thinking our parents are awesome and really did a pretty good job.

I know too that not everyone had a good experience as children and that their parents may have had difficulties in their relationship and that there may have been neglect. I am sorry if that is your story. I hope that someone though along the way filled that parent/mentor role for you. Whether an uncle/aunt, priest, teacher or coach. I reckon if you are sitting here today God provided someone to help get you where you are.

That is the love that John talks about in the second reading. The love that the Father has bestowed on us. We are all children of God and are called to love one another and remain in him. And how do we know that he remains with us? We know this because of the gift of the Holy Spirit that is given to us. His abiding presence in our life, our relationships and creation as we talked about at Christmas.

Mary and Joseph find Jesus after four days because the Spirit willed that to happen not because they did an exceptional job looking for him.

This feast is about love, the love of family, friends, community Gods love for us. That love can make us anxious, stressed, nervous even angry and betrayed. If we can surrender those difficult feelings, show the people in our lives love, the love of forgiveness and humility we will find peace and joy on the other side. We will recognize that maybe our folks didn't alway get it right but they tried and by the grace of God I am who I am and I need to do my best to share the love that God has bestowed on me.

This space is for you to record your comments or your groups comments

THE EPIPHANY OF
THE LORD - YEAR C

Is 60:1-6; Ps 72; Eph 3:2-3a,5-6; Mt 2:1-12

In many countries this is the day for exchanging gifts with family and friends - little Christmas it is often called. It certainly seems appropriate to me as we recognize that the Christ child was recognized by the Magi as the new born king of the Jews and they gave him gifts of gold, frankincense and myrrh.

Of course the Magi were not the first to greet the child. Depending on which Christmas Mass you went to you may have heard Luke's recount of the birth of Christ where by the angel of the Lord appeared to the shepherds in the field and told them where they could find the savior. So the shepherds were first. And these folks were really looked down upon by the establishment the Pharisees and scribes because their occupation often didn't allow them to practice the Jewish faith and it's rituals, the washing, the call to the synagogue on the sabbath for if they left there was no one to take care of their flock so they just worked.

But in this case they are not too far away and they can bring the lambs with them and they do and they are amazed at what they see. Jesus came to give them the lowly the oppressed the dominated, he came to give them hope and to tell them of Gods love for them.

As we know very few of those in power or the well to dos will recognize the Christ. The Magi clearly do but Herod and all the others will reject His message of love and kill him.

As I thought about those called and those not called by God I wonder why? Why does God call the Shepherds and the Magi but not Herod? I believe God IS calling them and all of us. The Magi clearly were"astrologers" and paid attention to what was going on around them they most likely prayed and heard their call.

The shepherds live a quiet life among the lambs and they were able to hear Gods angel in the quiet of the night. Paul as we hear in the second reading along with the apostles and the prophets hear God's calling for them because they are open to it.

They aren't just focused on their success, collecting things, money fame and fortune. They are focused on their families and their God and they hear the call and they respond.

The call of the Lord is happening today to all people. I am guessing if we are here that we have at least heard the call. But is our response just attending Mass each week? What do we do during the rest of the week?

It could be that our friends are not here because we are the angels of the Lord in their lives called to tell them about the Christ child, the savior the king. We can't keep this miracle to ourselves we have to share it, share the joy and the hope of what Christmas and epiphany mean. Our world is sad and broken. It needs the joy of the Lord.

Let us leave this place today like the shepherds and the Magi left Jesus, Mary and Joseph to return to their lives enriched by their encounter, let us too take our experience home and share it with those we meet this week. God is calling everyone and He may be doing it through us.

This space is for you to record your comments or your groups comments

THE BAPTISM OF
THE LORD - YEAR C

Is 42:1-4,6-7 OR Is 40:1-5, 9-11; Ps 29 OR Ps 104; Acts 10:34-38 OR Titus 2:11-14, 3:4-7; Lk 3:15-16, 21-22

Fast forward from last week with the nativity scene and the Magi recognizing Jesus as the new born King of the Jews and the wise men presenting him with all the gifts, Today we have God himself speaking to the people at the River Jordan being baptized where Jesus is now an adult.

Luke says "after all the people had been baptized and Jesus also had been baptized and was praying, heaven was opened and the Holy Spirit descended upon him in bodily form like a dove. And a voice came from heaven, "You are my beloved Son; with you I am well pleased.""

Few thoughts. Herod and the Pharisees were not present. The Romans were not present. It was the people being baptized by John who were present. It was the people who wanted a fresh start, wanted be more than what society told them what they were - peasants, slaves, worth nothing in the eyes of the Pharisees and the Romans.

And the first readings and second readings available to us today all talk about the same thing. Isaiah "my chosen one with whom I am well pleased will bring justice to the nations", "Comfort, give comfort to my people", from Acts Peter says "i see that God shows no partiality.. whoever acts rightly is acceptable", and finally Paul in his letter to Titus says "The grace of God (Jesus) has appeared saving all and training us to reject godless ways and worldly desires and to live temperately, justly and devoutly.. with hope".

Again those people were dominated by the ruling class, they were the ones that built the cities, worked the farms and clean the palaces. In the eyes of the ruling class they were nothing. But the readings tell us that they are something. We are all something regardless of what the world thinks of us! We are children of God.

So now that we know this how should we act? We need to act justly as Paul says to Titus says! We need to have hope and apply the teaching of Jesus - selflessness, be caring, giving, be nice!

It's really not that hard but we get caught up in the standards of the world. In the end none of that will matter. You will be remembered by your family and friends hopefully as someone who cared and helped and loved. They probably are not going to remember what car you drove - well maybe if you had a really cool car they might ☺ - and don't get me wrong - it's ok to have a cool car, I like cars but when those things of this world are the most important things then we haven't been listening, we don't get it.

God wants us to be happy and enjoy life but he wants that for everyone. And we are called by our Baptism to help God bring that happiness about , bring justice to the oppressed. Are you listening? How will you do that this week? Ask God what he needs you to do and he will tell you, he will present someone to you this week that you will be able to help. Just do it! Help them and by doing so you will be helping God bring about his Kingdom.

This space is for you to record your comments or your groups comments

ABOUT THE AUTHOR - ARMAND BRUNELLE

I am a computer scientist and entrepreneur. I go to Mass each weekend and on holy days. I am a cradle Catholic and was raised by two devout parents and grandparents.

I made the faith my own early in my 20s and began teaching catechism (Confirmation program grade 8 and 9) at 22 and continued to do so through 2021. My wife Michele and I spent 12 years doing youth ministry at our parish and then we had our own kids. We did our best to bring them up in the faith and I am happy to say they are active in practicing their Catholicism. I take no credit for that as I know many who have done the same things we did and their kids are not practicing. It is truly the grace of God.

Over the years I have done a lot of spiritual reading. I have a thirst to strengthen my relationship with God and it has been hard to quench. So I continue to read spiritual books as much as I can. One author stands out as my favorite and that is the Franciscan Father Richard Rohr. Some of you conservative Catholics may have just stopped reading and shut the book which would be unfortunate.

I read many of Father Rohr's books and took an online class with him on "The Alternative Franciscan Theology" I was able to join him on a retreat weekend in New Mexico. It was such a great prayerful weekend. After failing at contemplative prayer for many years, on that weekend I was given some tools and have had some success with it. Contemplative prayer is such a game changer. If you haven't spent time I would encourage you to do your best to figure it out. In fact, you can probably stop reading now as that is the biggest piece of advice I have for you. Go into the classroom of silence, listen and come to know God's love for you. It is simply awesome!

I would also list the following authors as having helped shape my thinking. In no particular order: Pope St. John Paull II, Pope Francis, Thomas Merton, Henri Nouwen, Julian of Norwich, Marcus Borg & John Dominic Crossan, James Martin, SJ, Walter Ciszek, SJ, Bishop Robert Barron, Matthew Kelly, William Paul Young. Each one has moved me further on the journey and encouraged me to seek Him further still. I thank them for their witness and only hope that perhaps in some small way I might be able to do the same for you here.

As each of us is called by our Baptism to evangelize the world and bring others to know God, I believe we must focus on God's abundant love and mercy that he has for us. We spend too much time in "Sin Management" as Rohr calls it and not enough time telling people that God loves them just as He created them. He wants a relationship with each one of us. I believe if more people come to know this then they will bring that love they receive from the Father into the world through love of neighbor. That will multiply upon itself and only then will we truly know peace in this world.

Visit my website at www.armandbrunelle.com